He was a year old when he made them.

Koalas have two thumbs on each hand.

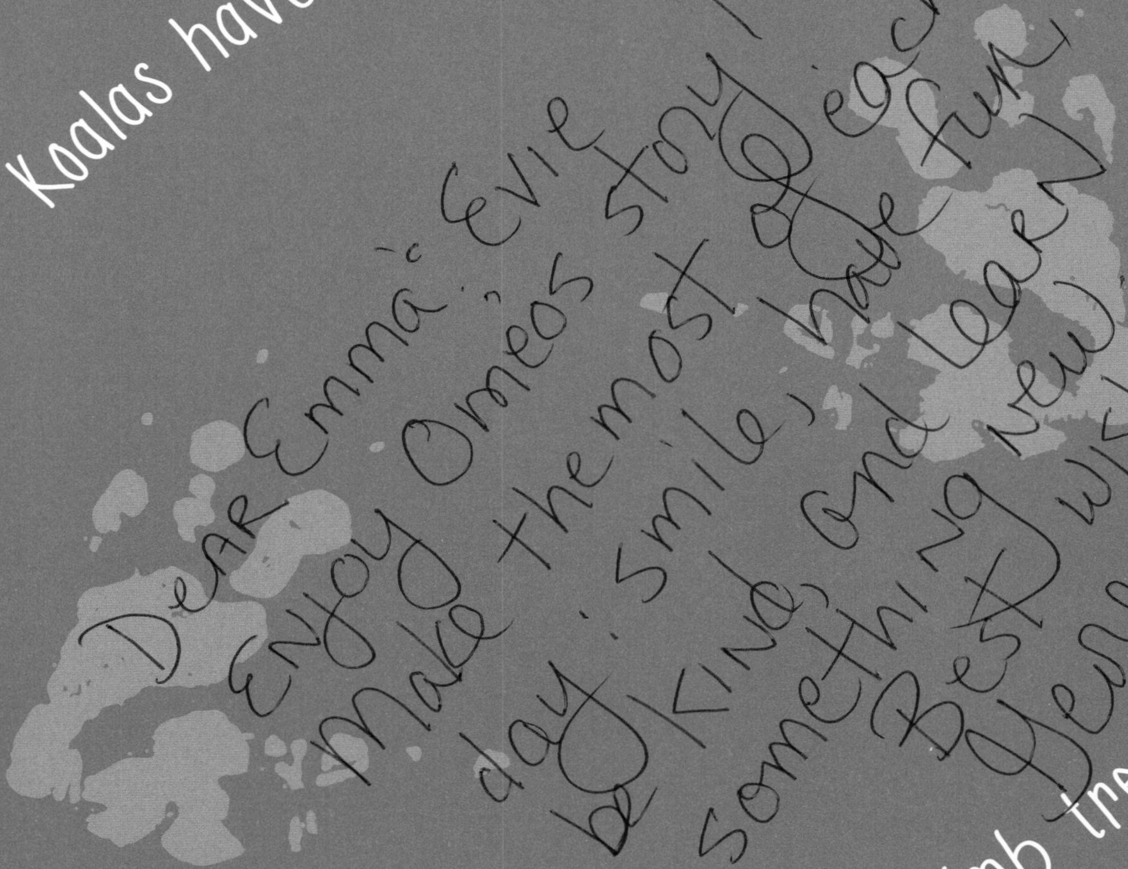

Dear Emma + Evie

Enjoy Omeos story!

Make the most of each

day; smile, have fun,

be kind, and learn

something new.

Best wishes

Georgeanne

Alvine

This helps them climb trees.

Amazing Omeo

A Baby Koala's True Story of Survival

Amazing Omeo: A Baby Koala's True Story of Survival was published by San Diego Zoo Wildlife Alliance Press in association with Blue Sneaker Press. Through these publishing efforts, we seek to inspire children and adults to care about wildlife, the natural world, and conservation.

San Diego Zoo Wildlife Alliance is a nonprofit international conservation leader, committed to inspiring a passion for nature and working toward a world where all life thrives. It supports cutting-edge conservation, and its work extends from San Diego to eco-regional conservation "hubs" across the globe.

Paul Baribault, President and Chief Executive Officer
Shawn Dixon, Chief Operating Officer
David Miller, Chief Marketing Officer
Georgeanne Irvine, Director of Publishing
San Diego Zoo Wildlife Alliance
P.O. Box 120551
San Diego, CA 92112-0551
sdzwa.org | 619-231-1515

San Diego Zoo Wildlife Alliance's publishing partner is Blue Sneaker Press, an imprint of Capen Publishing Company, Inc., 4440 Edison Street, San Diego, California, 92117.

Christopher G. Capen, President
Carrie Hasler, Publisher, Blue Sneaker Press
Kristin Connelly, Managing Editor
Lori Sandstrom, Art Director/Graphic Designer
capenpubco.com | 800-358-0560

ISBN: 978-1-943198-21-4
Library of Congress Control Number: 2023941568
Printed in China
10 9 8 7 6 5 4 3 2 1

To Omeo the koala,
whose will to live inspired me, and to
the veterinary team and wildlife care specialists
who helped Omeo survive and thrive.

Acknowledgments

THANK YOU TO THE FOLLOWING PEOPLE FOR HELPING BRING HOPE TO CHILDREN EVERYWHERE BY SHARING OMEO'S INSPIRATIONAL AND HEARTWARMING STORY:

Becky Kier; Cora Singleton, DVM; Lindsey King; Mary Dural; Kim Weibel; Zabrina Bohy; Courtney Roth; Chris Hamlin Andrus; Lisa Martin; Jennifer Roesler; Candis Malcolm; Jennifer Moll; Gaylene Thomas; Scott Rammel; Paul Baribault; Shawn Dixon; David Miller; Andrea McCallin; Lianne Hedditch; Darla Davis; Ken Bohn; Tammy Spratt; Lisa Bissi; Jen MacEwen; Kim Turner; Jennifer Tobey; Olivia Schouten; Christine Yetman; Peggy Scott; Carrie Hasler; Lori Sandstrom; Kristin Connelly; Meredith Ryan, FAWNA New South Wales; and Angel Chambosse.

PHOTO CREDITS:

Ken Bohn: 7 lower, 8, 9 upper, 10, 11, 22, 23 upper, 24, 25, 27 lower, 32, 33, 34 upper left, 34 lower left, back jacket flap.
Tammy Spratt: front cover, front jacket flap, title page, 12, 13 upper right, 15, 16, 18 upper, 19, 20.
Georgeanne Irvine: 3, 13 upper left, 14, 17, 18 lower, 21, 26, 27 upper, 30, 31, back cover. **San Diego Zoo Wildlife Care Team:** 28, 29.
Zabrina Bohy: 4, 9 lower. **Becky Kier:** 5 upper left. **Lindsey King:** 5 upper right. **San Diego Zoo Veterinary Services:** 23 lower.
Ron Garrison: 35 lower right. **Shutterstock—Anek Suwannaphoom:** 7 upper left; **Andras Deak:** 34 right inset;
Constantin Stanciu: 34 lower right; **slowmotiongli:** 35 lower left; **Paleokastritsa:** 36 upper; **Jimmy W.:** 36 lower;
Kaesler Media: 36 right inset. **Minden Pictures—D. Parer and E. Parer-Cook:** 6, 7 upper right.
iStock—John Carnemolla: 35 upper left; **iso100k:** 35 upper right. **Alamy—Gerry Pearce:** 35 center.

Rescuing a Baby Koala

"Squeak!" the nearly hairless baby koala squealed as wildlife care specialist Lindsey King gently cradled him in her hands. The tiny koala, called a joey, was only five months old and smaller than most koalas his age. Normally, a koala that young would still be in his mother's pouch, but his mother had just passed away after an illness. The wildlife care team at the San Diego Zoo would now be caring for him.

The koala joey's weight was just a little more than a baseball's, five and a half ounces.

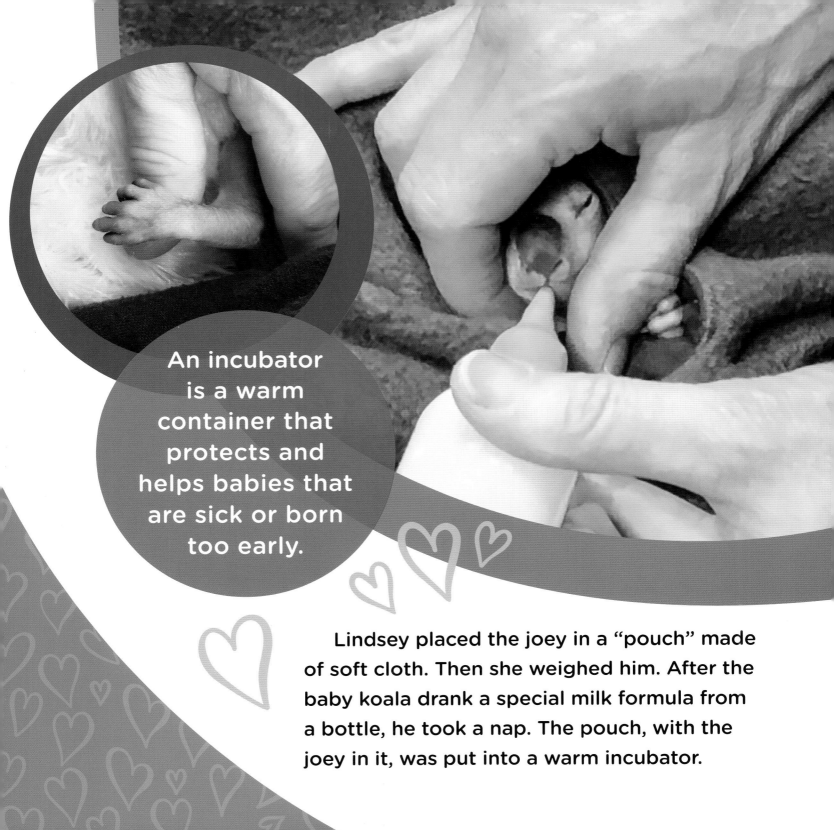

An incubator is a warm container that protects and helps babies that are sick or born too early.

Lindsey placed the joey in a "pouch" made of soft cloth. Then she weighed him. After the baby koala drank a special milk formula from a bottle, he took a nap. The pouch, with the joey in it, was put into a warm incubator.

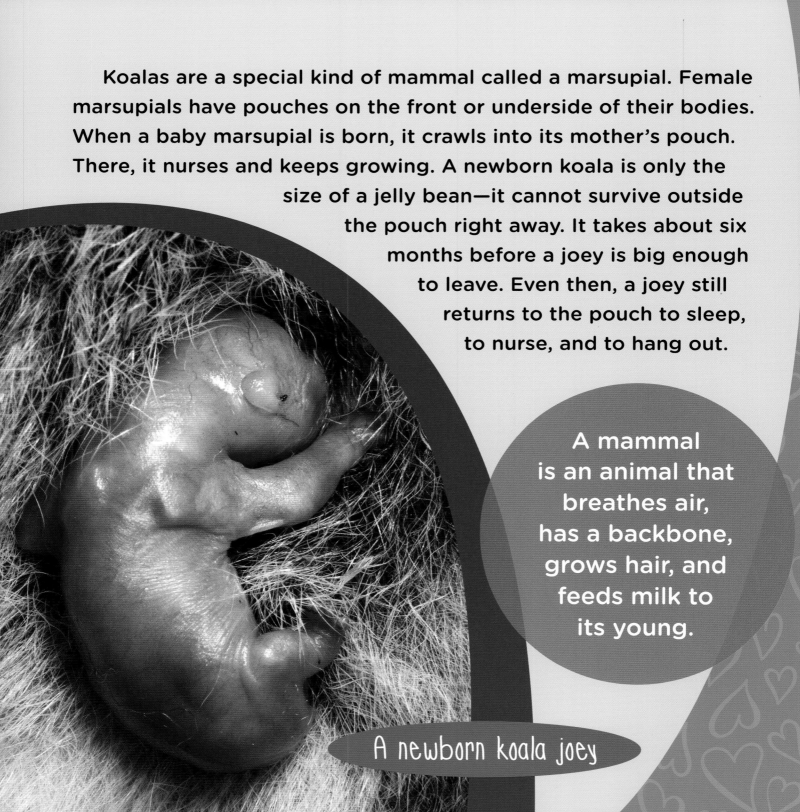

Koalas are a special kind of mammal called a marsupial. Female marsupials have pouches on the front or underside of their bodies. When a baby marsupial is born, it crawls into its mother's pouch. There, it nurses and keeps growing. A newborn koala is only the size of a jelly bean—it cannot survive outside the pouch right away. It takes about six months before a joey is big enough to leave. Even then, a joey still returns to the pouch to sleep, to nurse, and to hang out.

A mammal is an animal that breathes air, has a backbone, grows hair, and feeds milk to its young.

A newborn koala joey

Kangaroos and wombats are marsupials, too.

Zoo veterinarian Dr. Cora Singleton worried. Since the rescued koala was only five months old, she knew it was unlikely that a koala so young could survive without its mother's care.

A Roller Coaster Ride

The first two weeks outside of his mother's pouch were like a roller coaster. Sometimes the joey was hungry. Other times, he wouldn't eat. He seemed strong one day and then weak the next.

Because the joey was so young and tiny, there was a chance he could get sick.

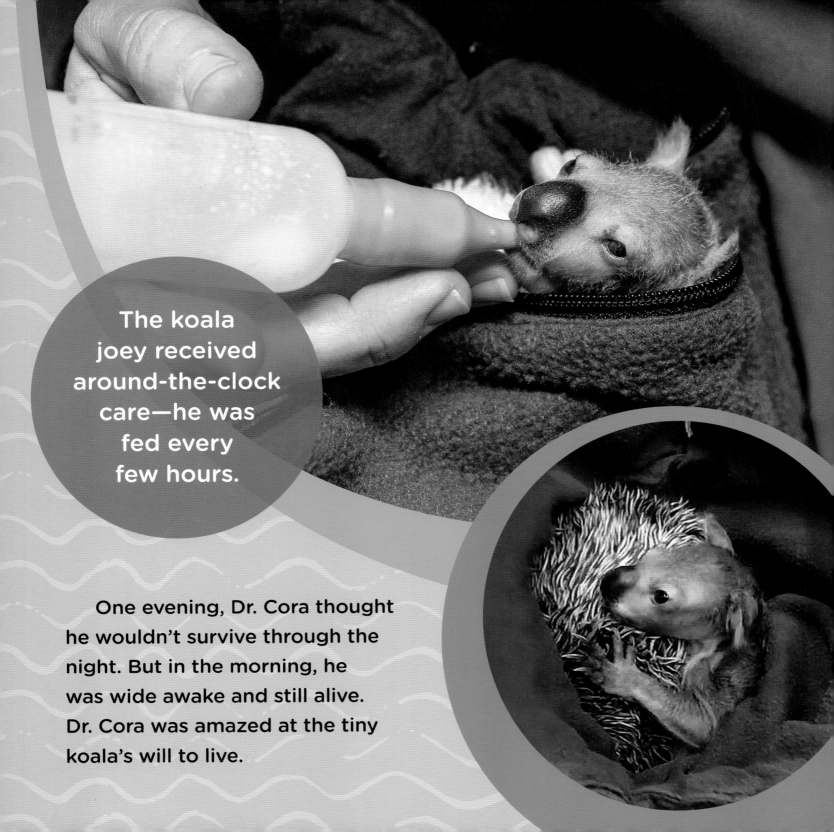

The koala joey received around-the-clock care—he was fed every few hours.

One evening, Dr. Cora thought he wouldn't survive through the night. But in the morning, he was wide awake and still alive. Dr. Cora was amazed at the tiny koala's will to live.

An Uphill Battle

One day during a bottle-feeding, a wildlife care specialist noticed the joey was having trouble breathing. Dr. Cora examined him and the news was not good: he had pneumonia.

Dr. Cora gave medicine to the tiny koala. She used a special tool called a nebulizer. It turned the medicine into a mist that he could breathe in through his nose. The veterinarian wasn't sure, though, that the koala would survive.

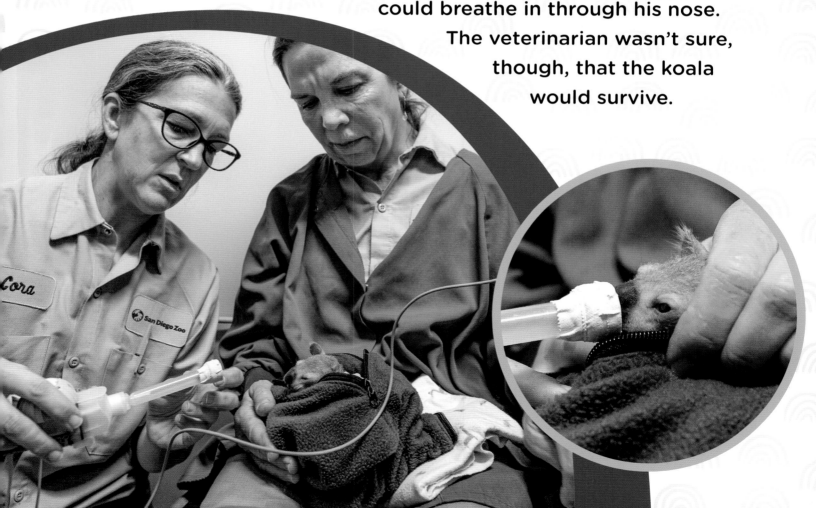

But the joey was a fighter! The medicine started to work, and the koala began getting better—and bigger—every day. Fur was beginning to grow on his head and body, and his teeth were coming in, too.

The baby was finally given a name: Omeo (Oh-me-oh), which is an indigenous Australian word that means "mountains" or "hills." It was the perfect name since Omeo had faced an uphill battle to survive.

The wildlife care team asked koala experts in Australia for advice when caring for Omeo.

Feeding Omeo

In the incubator, Omeo spent most of the time in his pouch, just like he would if he were still with his mother. Sometimes, he climbed out and snuggled up to a plush koala toy to help comfort him.

Omeo's bottle-feedings could be challenging for the wildlife care specialists. Getting him to drink out of the bottle wasn't easy! Omeo sometimes fussed and pushed the bottle out of his mouth, usually because he was full or he wanted his milk rewarmed.

When Omeo was tucked in his pouch and cuddled up to a plush toy, he was comfortable and relaxed. Then he would focus on his bottle and be a good eater.

Sun Time

Omeo spent more and more time out of his incubator and pouch as he got older. The wildlife care specialists made a short "tree" from branches, where they placed a koala plush. The plush was about the size of a koala mother. Omeo clung to the plush koala's back, just like other koala joeys cling to their moms. Omeo would crawl, climb, and explore when he was on his tree. This helped him get stronger.

Sun time started out at 10 minutes a day but got longer as Omeo grew older.

On sunny afternoons, Omeo was given "sun time" while he snuggled in his pouch. Being outdoors in the fresh air helped Omeo learn about the sights, sounds, and smells of the other koalas as well as the Zoo visitors.

Eucalyptus for Omeo

Although Omeo was still drinking from his bottle, his caregivers began giving him eucalyptus (yoo-kuh-lip-tus) leaves, the only food that adult koalas eat. Eucalyptus is poisonous to most animals but not to koalas! Koalas have special bacteria in their stomachs that allow them to eat it. Joeys get that bacteria by eating pap from their mothers. Pap is a type of koala poop that lets a koala mom pass good bacteria to her baby. But, without a mom, Omeo had to be fed pap from other koalas.

Bacteria are tiny organisms, or living things, that are found all throughout nature.

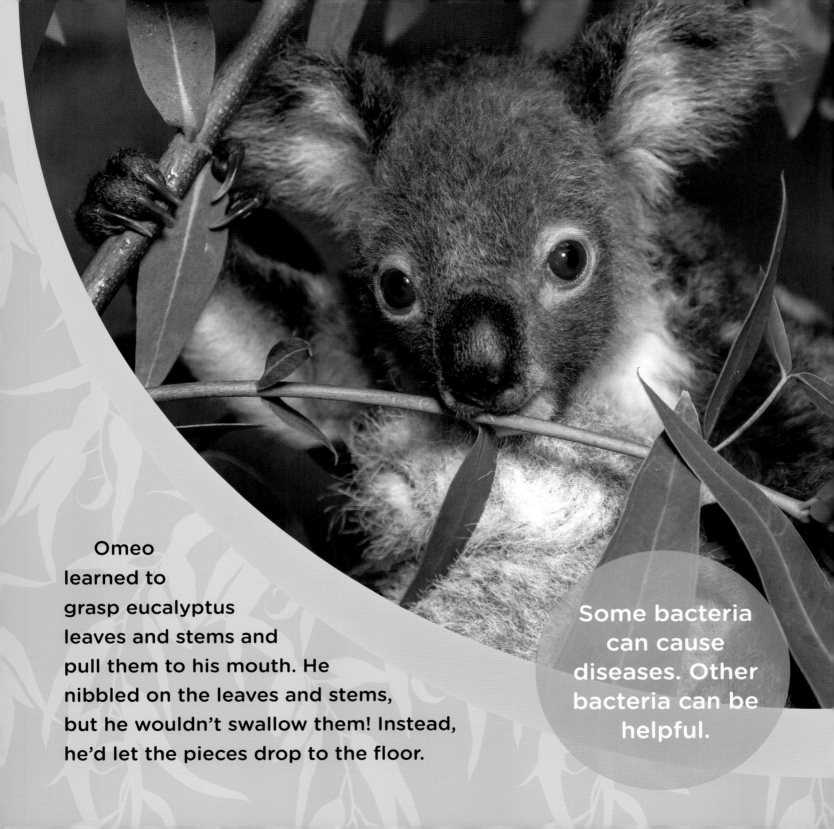

Omeo learned to grasp eucalyptus leaves and stems and pull them to his mouth. He nibbled on the leaves and stems, but he wouldn't swallow them! Instead, he'd let the pieces drop to the floor.

Some bacteria can cause diseases. Other bacteria can be helpful.

Visiting the Other Koalas

When Omeo was eight and a half months old, he didn't need to sleep in the incubator anymore. Instead, he stayed in an indoor area. There, Omeo was given fresh eucalyptus every day, but he would still only nibble it. By now, he should have been eating eucalyptus and not just drinking from his bottle. Maybe a visit with other koalas would help! The wildlife care team hoped the koalas might show him how to eat eucalyptus.

The Zoo grows about 30 types of eucalyptus for the koalas to eat.

Omeo was often carried to the koala habitat clinging to a plush koala. A real mother koala with a joey on her back climbed away. Another koala sniffed Omeo, but she wasn't interested in him. Cynthia the koala let Omeo climb on her back, but when he climbed on her head, she got annoyed.

And, even though Omeo saw the other koalas eating eucalyptus leaves, he would only swallow the stems and the bark . . . NOT the leaves!

All about Climbing

Spending time in the koala habitat was good for Omeo. He watched the other koalas eat eucalyptus leaves, and his climbing skills began to grow. He became braver and more confident. Omeo liked a challenge: if a branch seemed out of reach, he tried to climb up to it anyway. If there was a new area to explore, he headed over to take a look. Sometimes he climbed so high, he wasn't always sure how to get down. He either figured it out or the wildlife care specialists helped him down.

Time for a Checkup

At 10 months old, Omeo weighed a little more than two pounds. Most koalas that age weigh between three and four pounds. Dr. Cora was worried again. She decided to examine him to make sure he was healthy.

By 10 months old, koalas usually get most of their food from eucalyptus leaves, not from their mother's milk.

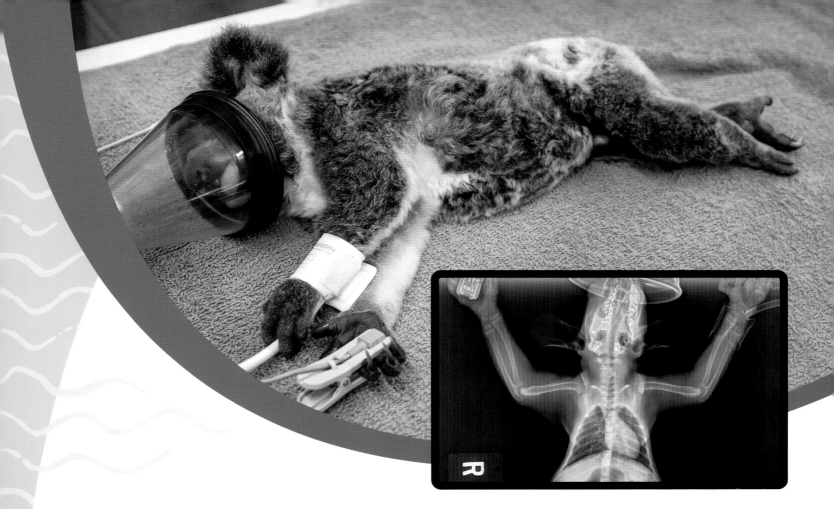

Omeo was carried into the Zoo hospital clinging to a plush toy to keep him relaxed. Then he was given medicine through a clear mask to make him sleep during his checkup. A few days before the exam, Omeo's wildlife care specialists helped him get used to the mask by putting it up to his face for short periods of time.

Dr. Cora took X-rays of Omeo's lungs, heart, and other organs. They looked good. She also examined his eyes, ears, and nose, and took a blood sample. Omeo was healthy, but Dr. Cora said he needed to start eating more eucalyptus leaves and drinking less milk.

Happy Birthday, Omeo!

July 15 was a big day for Omeo—it was his first birthday! It had been seven months since he lost his mother. There were many times the wildlife care team wasn't sure Omeo would survive. Yet now he was a year old! To celebrate, they made a cake out of ice shaped like a heart. It was filled with eucalyptus leaves and decorated with paperbark tree flowers.

Omeo just sniffed the cake, but he didn't eat any of it. Eventually, it melted.

Omeo first checked out his cake. Then he climbed along a big branch and jumped several feet to another one. The wildlife care specialists cheered—they were pleased and amazed that he could jump so far. Omeo was active for the rest of the morning. He showed off his athletic skills as he climbed high in the trees.

Weaning Omeo

Two months after Omeo's first birthday, Dr. Cora and the wildlife care team created a plan to wean him from his milk formula. When he became an adult, he needed to eat only eucalyptus leaves, not milk.

Weaning means getting a baby or young animal used to food other than milk.

They gave Omeo different kinds of eucalyptus to see what he liked best. He got fewer bottles each day. He also ate smoothies made from ground up eucalyptus leaves mixed with water and powdered milk formula. Omeo liked the smoothies. Maybe he would soon start to eat whole leaves!

Cameras were set up in Omeo's habitat. His caregivers could keep an eye on him from their computers. Omeo began eating leaves more often. He liked the thinner leaves better than the thick, waxy leaves, which are harder to chew. But Omeo still ate stems and bark, which aren't as good for him as leaves.

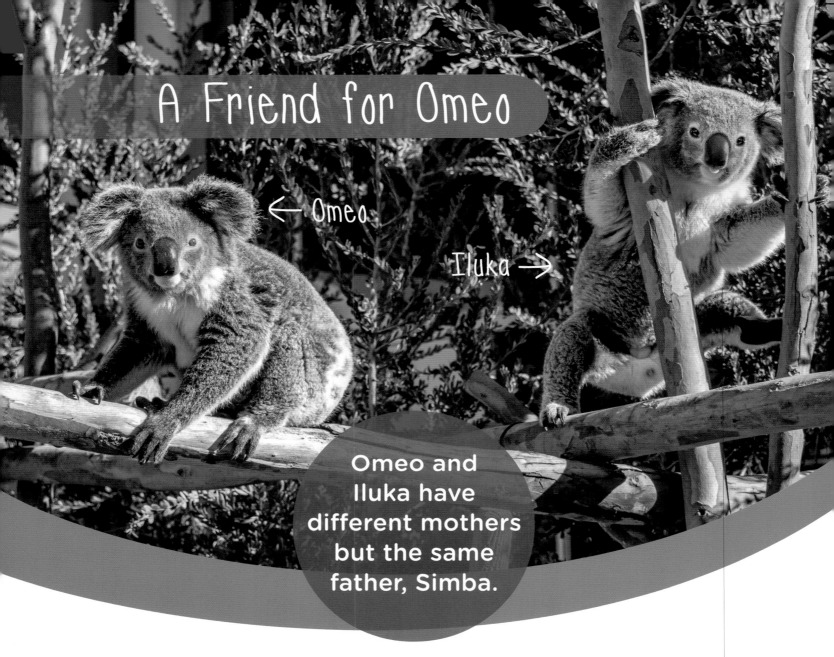

A Friend for Omeo

← Omeo

Iluka →

Omeo and Iluka have different mothers but the same father, Simba.

Part of the weaning plan was to introduce Omeo to Iluka (Eye-loo-kuh), his younger half brother. Iluka was already eating eucalyptus for all of his meals. He would hopefully show Omeo the best leaves to eat. Even though Omeo was three months older, he was smaller than Iluka.

At first, Omeo and Iluka didn't pay much attention to each other. But it didn't take them long to become buddies. Their friendship caused some challenges for Omeo, though. He was eating more leaves but not enough. While the koala brothers were together, Iluka always wanted to play. They climbed on, swatted at, and pushed each other. When it was time to eat, Iluka distracted Omeo.

Omeo wasn't eating—or resting—enough when he was with Iluka. The wildlife care specialists decided it was best for them to spend their time apart.

Omeo →

← Iluka

When male koalas become adults, they don't hang out together.

Poop Soup

One morning, Omeo's stomach began gurgling. He was also stretching and sitting up straight, which are signs of a tummy ache. X-rays showed that his stomach was filled with gas, which could be dangerous. The gas went away and Omeo got better, but his tummy ache kept coming back.

Lindsey took Omeo to the Zoo hospital for another checkup. Dr. Cora X-rayed his stomach again and gave him medicine to make him sleep. Lindsey stirred up a mixture of koala poop and water. The poop was from several koalas, including a mother with a six-month-old joey. This "poop soup" was like pap from a koala mother.

The stomach digests food by breaking it down and turning it into energy.

gas bubbles

With some help, Omeo stood in front of an X-ray machine so Dr. Cora could see inside his body.

Dr. Cora hoped the good bacteria from the other koalas' stomachs would be passed on to Omeo. The bacteria could help him digest leaves more easily.

Over the next few weeks, Omeo ate more and more leaves—and his stomach didn't hurt anymore. The poop soup had helped!

Omeo Thrives!

When Omeo celebrated his second birthday, Dr. Cora and the wildlife care specialists felt like they had received the best gift of all—Omeo was healthy, strong, and all grown-up.

Dr. Cora smiled as she watched Omeo on his special day! He had overcome many health challenges to the surprise of everyone. And now here he was—munching on a big number two made out of eucalyptus leaves and paperbark tree flowers.

No more bottle for Omeo! Just like other adult koalas, he now only eats eucalyptus leaves.

With the excellent care that he received—and his strong will to live—Omeo beat the odds and now is thriving at the San Diego Zoo. He brings joy to everyone who sees him and especially to all of the people—like Dr. Cora and the wildlife care team—who never gave up on saving his life.

Fun Facts about Koalas

Koalas are sometimes mistakenly called "koala bears," but they are not bears. They are marsupials.

Adult female marsupials carry their babies, called joeys, in pouches.

A baby koala is very tiny when it is born—about the size of a jelly bean! It then spends its first six months in its mother's pouch.

Koalas eat only eucalyptus leaves.

A joey often rides on its mother's back or belly when it gets too big for the pouch.

Koalas spend most of their time high up in eucalyptus trees, napping and eating.

Koalas get most of their water from eucalyptus leaves, but they will drink water when it's very hot and dry.

Koalas have fingerprints like primates and humans.

Koalas can sleep up to 20 hours a day.

Koalas have two toes that are fused together on their feet, which creates a double-clawed "toe" for grooming.

Koala is thought to mean "no drink" in several indigenous Australian languages.

A male koala has a scent gland on his chest, which looks like a bare patch of skin.

Koalas make sounds that include snores, bellows, and screams.

Where Koalas Live in the World

AUSTRALIA

KOALAS ARE ENDANGERED IN SOME AREAS OF AUSTRALIA, INCLUDING QUEENSLAND AND NEW SOUTH WALES.

Threats to Koalas

- Habitat loss: eucalyptus forests are being cleared for roads, homes, farms, and ranches.

- Being killed by motor vehicles and attacked by dogs: when their habitat is fragmented, koalas must travel on the ground and cross roads to get from one forest to another.

- Climate change, which causes more frequent and intense bushfires that destroy forests.

- Diseases.

How You Can Help

To learn how you can be an ally for koalas
and other wildlife as well as help the
San Diego Zoo Wildlife Alliance create a
world where all life thrives, visit

sdzwa.org

Ten Things You and Your Family Can Do to Help Wildlife:

1. Learn about the local wildlife that lives in or near your community.

2. Create your own wildlife habitat by planting native bushes, flowers, and trees in your yard. You can put up a bird feeder, too.

3. Keep your cats indoors so they stay safe and don't hurt local wildlife, such as birds, lizards, and small mammals.

4. Tell your friends and family not to purchase products made from threatened trees and plants, marine organisms, or wild animals when traveling abroad.

5. Put trash that can't be recycled in a garbage can so it doesn't end up harming wildlife or traveling to the ocean.

6. Recycle paper products, glass bottles, cans, and plastic, and say "no" to plastic bottles, straws, lids, and cutlery.

7. Use a reusable water bottle.

8. Take your own reusable bags to the grocery store.

9. Volunteer to be a "citizen scientist" on **wildwatchkenya.org** and **wildwatchburrowingowl.org** to help scientists identify wildlife in photos taken on trail cameras (with your parents' permission).

10. Find out more about how climate change is affecting our planet and share this information with the people in your life.